The Beauty of It All

Poems by

Pamela Martin

The Beauty of It All
Copyright 2007 by Pamela Gowan

All rights reserved under International and Pan-American copyright conventions. No part of this book may be reproduced, stored in a retrieval system or transmitted in any form, electronic, mechanical, or by any other means, without written permission of the author.

International Standard Book Number: 978-0-578-02297-0

Illlustrated by Kathleen Hardy.

Table of Contents

Part I

The Antiquary 11
Plagiarism vs. Pugilism 11
The Prince 11
Lazy Susan 12
Sine qua non 12
Mistaken Identity 12
The Wild, Wild West 13
"When" 13
Plan "B" Dexterous 13
Speakeasy 14
Tabloid Tabloids 14
Salutary Neglect 14
Abstruse Recluse 15
Lazy Boy 15
Lady Luck 15
Pax Romana 16
Urine Town 16
Jane Doe 16
Extreme Anonymity 17
Typical 17
Hard to Please 17
The Language Barrier 18
The *Alpha* and *Omega* 18
Idee Fixe 18
Polyanna Pam 19
Boundaries 19
Helen of Baghdad 19
Priceline 20
Stranger than Fiction 20
Growing Pains 20
Mrs. Robinson 21
Extreme Unction 21
A Most Difficult Choice 21

Part II

The *Only* Way to Go 25
Rewind 25
The Gift That Keeps on Giving...25
Venetian Gardens 26
R.L.S 26
Seurat 26
Semantics 27
Clairvoyant..27
Wunderkind...27
Candle in the Wind...28
Meditation on Life 28
The Hoax...28
T.G.I.F 29
When the Chips are Down 29
Make Haste Slowly 29
Ave Maria..30
Frequent Fryers 30
Politics as Usual...30
Peroration...31
The Interloper..31
Oncology...31
Secular Humanism 32
Platitudes-a-Plenty 32
"Save Me"...32
Free Will..33
Masonic Temple 33
Where the Boys Are 33
Depth Perception...34
Homily 34
Flee, Bag!..34
The Enablers 35
The Concession 35
A Night Mare 35

Part III

Rules of Disengagement 39
Dr. Philistine 39
Guilty as Sin 39
The Eternal Present 40
Los Alamos 40
Be Happy! 40
The Palliative 41
Coping Mechanisms 41
A Spotless Reputation 41
The leopard does not change his spots 42
Side by Side 42
Oddball 42
Just Because 43
Classical Beauty 43
An Eleusinian Mystery 43
Mad as a Hatter 44
Animalia 44
Dream Catcher 44
Tchotchkes 45
Expect the Unexpected 45
Primavera 45
Faint Praise 46
Ho-hum 46
Sam's Club 46
Simon Legree 47
Press Release 47
Half-Time 47
Escritoire 48
Having It All 48
Yellow Journalism 48
Do Not Resuscitate! 49
Lamb Chops 49
Seditious Libel 49
O Tannenbaum! 50

Part I

The Antiquary

Old friends make the best friends.
I am ninety-two.
If age is a mindset,
Then mine is set on you.
There's no fool like an old fool.
I know this is true.
I'm older now but wiser.
Let's just play it cool.

Plagiarism vs. Pugilism

Plagiarism and pugilism
Always end the same.
But no matter how you slice it,
No one is to blame.
A writer and a fighter
Have so much to prove.
Often they lose sight
Of what they have to lose.

The Prince

Lorenzo, the Magnificent,
Was known for his munificence
And depraved indifference
To the court of law.
It fell to him to do those things
We know are wrong but goodness brings
And for which the angel sings.
The beauty of it all.

Lazy Susan

Chronic ergophobia
Is the curse of man.
A woman can be dilatory
If she don't give a damn.
But one thing is for certain
It's a Judas kiss
When somebody tells you
Indolence is bliss.

Sine qua non

Confetti always makes me laugh.
Onions make me cry.
Catharsis is the sort of thing
That really gets me high.
Water is essential.
Oxygen is, too.
But the one thing I can't live without
Is my dear friend, you.

Mistaken Identity

Never was I
A recidivistic bride.
I had too much sense.
I had too much pride.
But if ever I am,
I say to you
We all make mistakes.
You've made a few.

The Wild, Wild West

Before the west was won
It was really wild.
It wasn't the kind of place
For the meek and mild.
Each man for himself
Was the golden rule.
Each man for himself.
Now it seems so cruel.

"When"

Tickle me tummy.
Tickle me chin.
Tickle me all over.
It ain't no sin.
Tickle me easy
Again and again.
Tickle me until
I say, "When."

Plan "B" dexterous

I am plan "B" dexterous
When it comes to you
Because in my heart
I know I have to
Rise to the occasion
Out of the blue.
Wherever I'm needed
I follow my cue.

Speakeasy

In the world of taciturnity
There's not much to say.
And I know for certain
We're better off that way.
In the world of volubility
More is said than done
About the things others do
When they're having fun.

Tabloid Tabloids

Gossip is the sort of thing
You should not believe
Unless you know for certain
You are not deceived.
Every rumor has a single
Point of origin
Which can never be destroyed
Much to our chagrin.

Salutary Neglect

Criminally negligent,
I have never been.
My mother always taught me
Negligence is sin.
But sometimes when I think about
How vigilant you are
I can't help but wonder
What you're doing in this bar.

Abstruse Recluse

You know I am erudite
When I wield my pen.
And I can be cryptic
As I befuddle them.
Esoteric I will ever be
If I have my way.
But who will understand
A single word I say?

Lazy Boy

Ergophobia and ergonomics
Are words that start the same.
Ergo I must say to you
Use their formal name.
One means you are lazy,
Lazy as a lout.
The other means you are comfy
When you get stressed out.

Lady Luck

You must risk a little to get a lot.
This is your lucky day.
If I knew then what I know now.
It wouldn't end this way.
You're free to choose. You snooze you lose.
I regret to say
If I knew then what I know now,
I would have run away.

Pax Romana

If peace be war and war be peace,
Miracles would never cease.
But when tempers flare and time is short,
Peace will be a last resort.

Urine Town

Public urination
Is the insubordination
That bears the designation
Of a criminal offense.
But gravity is the force
That lets nature run its course.
With all due remorse
That is my defense.

Jane Doe

Jane was a deer
Who lost her way.
And she was found dead
The very next day.
Who she was
Nobody knew.
Please, be advised
This could happen to you.

Extreme Anonymity

I am so anonymous
I don't know my name.
But one thing is for certain,
I take it not in vain.
If anyone should ask me
Why it is this way,
I simply smile and tell him
Some things I just can't say.

Typical

A lagniappe is a gratuity.
A gratuity is a tip
To insure promptness
With a little zip.
Should perchance you leave one,
Try to make it big
Because for all you know
It may be his only gig.

Hard to Please

You are so fastidious.
You always make a fuss
About the things we say and do
Just the two of us.
I hate to say I told you so
But sad to say it's true.
There's no one more crotchety
Than my dear friend, you.

The Language Barrier

When I ordered oatmeal,
I got eggs instead.
This was disconcerting
Because I clearly said
That I wanted oatmeal,
Oatmeal and some KLIM
(That's milk spelled backwards).
What was wrong with him?

The *Alpha* and *Omega*

Kodiak begins and ends
With the letter 'K."
Aria begins and ends
With the letter 'A."
My life begins and ends
With the letter 'U'
Because you are so dear to me.
Love me, love me do.

Idee Fixe

Obsessively compulsive
Is an *idée fixe*.
It's bad luck through an through
Like a triple six.
It dominates the mind
And permeates the soul
And tells us who we are
As if we didn't know.

Pollyanna Pam

I'm no Emily Procter
But I can say to you
It really doesn't matter
If you're feeling blue.
While feeling blue is something
That can happen to you,
It is always something
You can get used to.

Boundaries

Boundaries are for lovers
Who turn off the light
And share the same values
And do that which is right.
But boundaries aren't for lovers
Who love to pillow fight
And love to love each other
Every single night.

Helen of Baghdad

As a weapon of mass destruction,
I must say to you
You need look no further
To find a bigger fool.
But in the final analysis,
You must carry on
In pursuit of your Helen of Baghdad
Within the Pentagon.

Priceline

I'm living in a house of cards,
A castle made of sand,
A cross between the Wizard of Id
And a smoldering wasteland.
But if these accommodations don't suit you,
All that I can say
Is try Paris Hilton
Or find some fresh-cut hay.

Stranger Than Fiction

I am the perfect stranger,
Stranger than you know,
Stranger than a surfer boy
Surfing in the snow
But more perfect than an angel,
An angel dressed in white,
Who dances around inside your head
Bathed in a soft light.

Growing Pains

They're coming tomorrow to pick me up
And whisk me on my way
Back to where it all began,
Where I'll always stay.
How is it I look back
When forward I must go?
Because you must know where you've been
If you are to grow.

Mrs. Robinson

The cougar is on the prowl
Ready for a kill.
She tells him that he's her best friend,
That he makes time stand still.
Tempus fugit always!
But in all ways "Seize the Day!"
Age really doesn't matter
If love is here to stay.

Extreme Unction

Sugar Dads and Sugar Babies
Form symbiotic pairs.
He needs her and she needs him.
They cancel out their cares.
But before you rush to judgment,
As Dr. Phil has said,
Worse things could certainly happen.
You could turn up dead.

A Most Difficult Choice

When your thumb is green and your grass is not,
It's time to buy a flower pot.
But the time is now to end this ruse.
A flower pot is hard to choose.

Part II

The *Only* Way to Go

Death by misadventure
Is the oldest known to man.
Accidents do happen
On sea or air or land.
If someone should tell you
This cannot be so,
You just smile and tell them
It's the *only* way to go.

Rewind

In this land of second chances
The second time around
Is better than the first, they say,
To take away your frown.
So, listen up, you knuckleheads,
When you're feeling sad
Just close your eyes and recreate
The best sex you've ever had.

The Gift That Keeps on Giving

Re-gifting is something
Our family does a lot.
It starts with a gift
We should not have got
And ends in a pile
Of truly thoughtless gifts
But it's something we look forward to
Like continental drifts.

Venetian Gardens

Living in a trailer park
Is like living off the land
With precious few amenities
In a wonderland.
You wake up in the morning
At the crack of dawn
But I can't help but notice
You haven't got a lawn.

R.L.S.

I am Dr. Jekyll.
You are Mr. Hyde.
This much is for certain
We must now decide
Who is to be responsible
For what is said and done
In the name of science
If you and I are one.

Seurat

I once was lost but now am found.
It's as if I almost drowned.
But I'm glad to say I did not.
You silly boy connect the dots.

Semantics

A picture is worth ten thousand.
I'm at a loss for words
Not the kind you speak out loud,
The kind that can't be heard.
Non-verbal is the language
That cannot be said
Via the auditory nerves
Deep within your head.

Clairvoyant

A friend of mine is going blind
But sees more than I do.
A friend of mine divines divines
Within the walls of Belleview.
But, you my friend, make no mistake,
See the future clear
Especially when it comes to things
That to me are dear.

Wunderkind

When a child cries,
I cry a little, too.
When an actor acts,
I act a little, too.
But when a child acts,
There's not much I can do
Except wonder at the prodigy
That, my child, is you.

Candle in the Wind

I'm obsessed with my celebrity.
Everyone knows my name.
I love the paparazzi.
Such is the price of fame.
But to any and all who choose it
Stardom is a flame
That burns brightly only
If you play the game.

Meditation on Life

Wanton speculation
Is the bane of man
But one thing is for certain
I do the best I can
To make sense of this world,
This world in which we live.
Perhaps it's just as well.
I have so much to give.

The Hoax

He wired me the money.
I wired him the PIN
To access the account
That would not let him in.
You should really get insurance
When you lay your money down.
There's no use in pretending
It will take away that frown.

T.G.I.F.

If Christ had been an oenophile
He would have picked a wine
More suited to the circumstances
Of his place and time.
A simple wine decanter
Could have served him very well
And would have changed his disposition
As he waited for the knell.

When the Chips are Down

A chip on the shoulder.
A chip off the block.
Ruffles have ridges.
I keep 'em in stock.
But the ones made of chocolate
I simply adore.
Such is thy richness.
Can I have some more?

Make Haste Slowly

Instant gratification
Permeates our time.
This I-want-it-now attitude
Really is a crime.
Wait is now a four letter word,
Patience but a scorn.
If anybody's listening,
We need to reform.

Ave Maria

Mary was the mother of God
And she was his friend.
She stood by him through thick and thin
Until the bitter end.
Who would think that such a thing
Would be necessary?
Hail, Mary! You were there
To help write his obituary.

Frequent Fryers

The chicken crossed the road, it seems,
To get to the other side
But was killed by a poultry truck
In an apparent suicide.
A service was held in the hatchery
Where it could not be denied
Another chicken had flown the coop
To keep from being fried.

Politics as Usual

If I were elected president
Of the United States,
I would take the side
Of those with lesser fates.
It would be my duty
To do the best I can
To ameliorate the condition
Of each and every man.

Peroration

There is no rhyme or reason
To what we say or do.
It goes without saying
You would say it, too.
It goes without saying
We are out of touch.
It goes without saying
I have said too much.

The Interloper

He came in through the doggy door
And crawled across the kitchen floor
Like a hungry predator
At the break of day.
When he realized what he had done
He turned away and began to run
Brandishing his Tommy gun
Laughing all the way.

Oncology

Money doesn't grow on trees
But grows instead like a disease
That no doctor can appease
But still it is the answer
To lack of food and deprivation
Excessive want and desperation
Greed and lust and dissipation.
But still it is a cancer.

Secular Humanism

Life is but a master seed
That grows into a tender reed.
But like the gentle, fragile flower
It dies a little every hour.
Yet life moves forward as we speak
Flowing from the ancient Greeks.
It matters not what life is.
What matters is that we have lived.

Platitudes-a-Plenty

Heart of hearts, I love thee well.
I love you more than words can tell.
I love you more than you love me.
I love you for what you can be.
I love you, heart, for you are mine
And will stand the test of time.
Heart of hearts, I say to you
To myself I must be true.

"Save Me"

I want to be an "Easter Lily."
Won't you pray for me?
If you put me on your prayer list,
You will surely see
That I am worthy of your devotion
And your loving care
And, in the end, I might be
The answer to your prayers.

Free Will

They did their best to cleanse the air
Of misery and God's despair
But only made us more aware
That we must set the goal.
We emerged triumphantly
Stronger now that we can see
There exists the possibility
Of freedom of the soul.

Masonic Temple

Brick by brick, they tell you,
Build it they will come.
Make it high and mighty
Second best to none.
And when you are finished
It will last and last,
A constant reminder
Of the greatness of the past.

Where the Boys Are

The boys are where the girls are
Everybody knows.
Girls only come alive
When there's sand between their toes.
There's usually a good woman
Underneath your nose.
So follow every footprint
To see where it goes.

Depth Perception

The older I get, the less I remember.
The less I remember, the more I forget.
The more I forget, the more I perceive
That what really matters is what we believe.

Homily

Every cloud has a silver lining
And a golden parachute.
And no matter how you slice it,
Eat a lot of fruit.
Only good comes of kindness.
Always hate hate.
Love is a form of blindness
And so is fate.

Flee, Bag!

Excema and seborrhea
Psoriasis and diarrhea
I got them all at Casa Mia
In a Tuscan town.
Take my advice.
Stay somewhere nice.
Don't quibble at the price.
It will bring you down.

The Enablers

Astrology explains
Why we fall in love.
We are assisted in this matter
By the skies above.
Youth and inexperience
Have gotten us this far.
The rest, as they say,
Is written in the stars.

The Concession

When we go to see a movie,
We always get popcorn.
It helps to pass the time
Especially if it's porn.
Only divine intervention
Could make me believe
That what they put before me
Is only make-believe.

A Night Mare

My flashlight is so tiny
It hardly makes a light.
What will I do
In the middle of the night?
Fumble around blindly
Missing every mark
Or simply get a horse
That can see in the dark?

Part III

Rules of Disengagement

If I move in with you
And you move in with me
We would come to live
In perfect harmony.
But when things get stale,
As they often do,
Just blame it on me
And I'll blame it on you.

Dr. Philistine

Dr. Phil is full of it
Which is apropos.
He specializes in vignettes
And endless tales of woe.
We watch him almost every day.
We rarely miss his show
Filled with patronizing insights
We already know.

Guilty as Sin

Probable cause
And reasonable doubt
Are what is left
When the jury is out.
Take your chances
And go to trial.
Maintain your innocence.
Stay in denial.

The Eternal Present

We are in the moment,
In the here and now,
Living free and easy
Making it somehow.
Life goes on without us.
Be that as it may.
There's really nothing wrong
With living for today.

Los Alamos

The saddest occasions
Are the ones made by man
Manufactured always
By his sleight of hand.
Harnessing the atom
Quickly comes to mind
As a defining moment
In the history of mankind.

Be Happy!

Be bold and be beautiful.
Be all you can be.
Always be yourself
And you'll always be free.
Be good and be careful,
And ultimately
When you achieve nirvana,
You'll be happy!

The Palliative

Variety is the spice of life.
Some like it hot.
And some like it mild, they say.
And some like it not.
Diversity is another thing.
It's the new melting pot,
A racial panacea
That promises a lot.

Coping Mechanisms

There's a solution to every problem
And a problem to every solution.
There's pollution in every purity
And purity in every pollution.
But there's no hope in despair
And no despair in hope.
There's only the will to live
And the ability to cope.

A Spotless Reputation

The slightest impropriety
Can bring on notoriety
In polite society
Experience has shown.
So, take my advice
Give up every vice
And play it nice
If you live alone.

The leopard does not change his spots

Rats are neophobic.
I think I am, too.
I embrace the past
While rejecting all that's new.
I abhor the unfamiliar
But love the tried and true.
Sometimes moving forward
Is the hardest thing to do.

Side by Side

We must recognize
That you are not my type.
But such a revelation
Is little more than hype.
Winners have their circle.
Losers have their pride.
No matter if you win or lose
God is on your side.

Oddball

We went to see a creature feature
With my old English teacher
Who is now a distinguished preacher
Doing it for God.
But she was frightened by the plot,
So much so that she forgot
To close her eyes when she was shot
Which was rather odd.

Just Because

A way with words.
A turn of phrase.
We thought it
Was just a phase.
But life goes on
And so it was.
She got better
Just because.

Classical Beauty

What is more barbaric
Than cutting your own hair?
What is more Platonic
Than the perfect square?
What could be more beautiful
Than the swaying of the trees
Except perhaps the writings
Of Aristophanes?

An Eleusinian Mystery

From a blank page
I must proceed
Following closely
Where my muse leads.
How I get there
Starting from here
Is anyone's guess.
This much is clear.

Mad as a Hatter

I went to anger management.
It really made me mad
To think that it might only
Be a passing fad.
Anger is a sickness
But when managed well
Can make method out of madness
More than words can tell.

Animalia

There was lovely starfish
Lying on the beach .
It had washed ashore that morning
But was slightly out of reach.
Oh, to be a starfish!
Living in the sea.
He who made this little star
Was also who made me.

Dream Catcher

I have said enough, it seems,
To break your spirit and quash your dreams.
But you may be the lucky one
Because your life has just begun.
They say you have that new car smell,
And that you're doing very well
At what you do. What do you do?
Only you can make your dreams come true.

Tchotchkes

I apologize for all I've said
And most of what I've done.
But I will not apologize
For having too much fun.
Fun, they say, is the only thing
Money cannot buy.
That's not to say in any way
You should give up before you try.

Expect the Unexpected

My lava lamp sits quietly
On my chest of drawers.
I turn it on occasionally
But I simply can't ignore
That if the lava flows too quickly,
I may be consumed
By the lava in the lava lamp
And may not be exhumed.

Primavera

When it snows in April
It must be a fluke,
An outright freak of nature
Or fallout from a nuke.
Is this global warming?
It is just as well.
When it snows in April,
It is cold as hell.

Faint Praise

Putting Shakespeare in a box
May seem rather cruel
But not to those who know him
As a fossil fuel.
While volumes can speak volumes,
This shoebox is too small
To honor William Shakespeare
And give to him our all.

Ho-hum

Imus called them "nappy."
I called Don a "Ho."
Santa got probation
For shouting, "Ho! Ho! Ho!"
Christmas will not be the same
For you and, yes, for me.
We'll be lucky in the end
To have a [bleeping] crèche.

Sam's Club

I love kitty.
I love cat.
I love Sammy
As a matter of fact.
Sammy loves me.
I'm so small.
Sammy loves me
Most of all.

Simon Legree

There's a place in the world
For a man who does not work.
It's called the unemployment line
Unless he goes berserk.
And, while self-employment
May be a reality for some,
It remains an illusive dream
For almost everyone.

Press Release

Pretty kitties are best.
I have two.
Have to what?
I haven't a clue.
I have to tell you,
What can I do?
I have two kitties.
This much is true.

Half-Time

He captivated the audience
With his marching band.
They played so well I could tell
Why Sousa is so grand.
I often wonder to myself
How do they play and stand?
It's easy to do in review.
They practice in the sand.

Escritoire

Without paper, without pen.
How can we go on?
Computers really help us, though,
When we turn them on.
But technology per se
Can only go so far
When it comes to helping someone
Catch a falling star.

Having It All

You can't have it both ways
Or can you?
Can you have your cake
And eat it, too?
If I had the answer,
I wouldn't tell you
Unless you signed up
For Seminar II.

Yellow Journalism

Three kittens in a litter box
Were doing number one.
It was a match made in heaven
If ever there was one.
The contest was to see
Who would finish first
And was published as an expose
By William Randolph Hearst.

Do Not Resuscitate!

There's no better friend
Than the TV Guide.
It tells you what to watch
As if your brain has died.
A real friend wouldn't do this
To another friend.
A real friend would tell you
This is the end.

Lamb Chops

"I did nothing,"
said the innocent man.
"I am innocent,"
Said the Roman.
"I'm guilty as charged,"
I coldly confessed,
"But if I stay here,
I'll corrupt all the rest."

Seditious Libel

Those who cannot remember the past
Are destined to repeat it.
And those who repeat the past
Are destined to condemn it.
But those who condemn the past
Always have their reasons
Citing most often
The high incidence of treasons.

O Tannenbaum!

Sometimes I sit and wonder
At the foolish things I do.
But I know in my heart
You would do them, too.
With God as my witness
No one can deny
There's nothing stranger than fiction
Except a Christmas tree in July.

www.ingramcontent.com/pod-product-compliance
Lightning Source LLC
LaVergne TN
LVHW011431080426
835512LV00005B/378